AF226138

INFORMATION

FOR

ALEXANDER WEDDERBURN of *St. Germains*, Esq; and others, Defenders,

AGAINST

Sir Peter Halket *of* Pitfirran, *Baronet, and his Curator* ad litem, *Purfuers.*

SIR *Peter Wedderburn* of *Gosford* intermarried with Mrs. *Janet Halket* of *Pitfirran*, of which Marriage there was Iffue, feveral Children, Males and Females.

Of this Date, the faid Dame *Janet Halket*, with Advice and Confent of the faid Sir *Peter Wedderburn*, her Hufband, executed a Deed of Settlement or Tailzie of her proper Eftate of *Pitfirran*, and thereby granted Procuratory, for refigning the fame, in Favours, and for new Infeftment, to be granted in favours of herfelf and her faid Hufband, and longeft Liver of them, in Liferent, and to *Peter Wedderburn*, (afterwards Sir *Peter Halket*) in Fee, and the Heirs male and female of his Body; which failing, to *Charles Wedderburn*, their fecond lawful Son, and the Heirs male and female of his Body; which failing, to the other younger Sons procreated, or to be procreated of the faid Marriage, in their Order of Seniority, and the Heirs male and female of their refpective Bodies; which failing, to the Daughters procreated, or to be procreated of faid Marriage, in their Order of Seniority, and

9 Sept. 1706.

A   the

the Heirs male and female of their respective Bodies ; which failing, to a Series of other Substitutes, therein mentioned, with and under the Provisions, Conditions, and Irritancies, therein after specified.

Proviso 1st, " That the said *Peter Wedderburn*, and the o-
" ther Heirs of Tailzie and Provision, above written, shall be
" holden and obliged to assume, carry, and bear the Sirname,
" Title, Cognizance, Arms, and Coat-armorial of *Halket* of
" *Pitfirran*, wherein if they fail, the Person Failer, or Con-
" traveener, *and the Heirs of the said Contraveener's Body*, shall,
" *ipso facto*, amit, lose, tyne, and forfeit the said Lands and
" Estate, *simpliciter*, without any Necessity of Declarator for
" that Effect, and the said Lands and Estate shall incontinent
" thereafter devolve, accresce and pertain to the next Heir of
" Tailzie, above written, substitute to the Contraveener, and
" the Heirs of the Contraveener's Body, *&c.*"

Proviso 2d, " And because, by virtue of the Bond of Tail-
" zie of the said Sir *Peter Wedderburn*, his Lands and Barony
" of *Gosford*, and others, of the Day and Date of these Pre-
" sents, the same are thereby provided to the said *Charles Wed-*
" *derburn*, our second Son, and the Heirs of his Body ; which
" failing, to the other Heirs of Tailzie and Provision, therein
" specified, whereby it may happen, the said Estates of *Gos-*
" *ford* and *Pitfirran*, and Right of Succession thereto, to fall,
" devolve, and coincide in one and the same Person ; and it
" being my Intention, and the Intention of my said Husband,
" in the respective Tailzies of said Estates, to preserve the said
" Family and Estate of *Pitfirran*, separate and distinct from
" the said Estate and Family of *Gosford*, so long as there shall
" happen to be more than one Descendant of the Bodies of
" me and my said Husband existing on Life, at the Time of
" the said Union ; therefore, it is hereby specially provided
" and declared, that, in case the said Estates shall happen to
" coincide, and be united in the Person of the said *Charles Wed-*
" *derburn,*

" *derburn*, our said second lawful Son, without Heirs male or
" female of his Body, then, and in that Case, it shall be in
" the Option and Election of the said *Charles Wedderburn*, ei-
" ther to keep, hold and retain his Right and Possession of
" the said Estate of *Gosford*; in which Case, he shall be
" holden and obliged to denude himself, *omni habili modo*, of
" the said Estate of *Pitfirran*, in favours of *James Wedderburn*,
" his immediate younger Brother-german, and the other
" Heirs of Tailzie and Provision substitute to him, with and
" under the haill Conditions and Provisions contained in this
" present Tailzie; or otherwise, it shall be leisome to the said
" *Charles*, to enter to the Right and Possession of the said E-
" state of *Pitfirran*, by virtue of this present Tailzie; in which
" Case he shall be holden and obliged to denude himself of the
" said Estate of *Gosford*, Rents, Mails and Duties thereof,
" from the Time of the Succession foresaid, in favours of the
" said *James Wedderburn*, and the other Heirs substitute to him
" in the aforesaid Tailzie of said Estate, under the haill Con-
" ditions therein contained, and shall be holden and obliged to
" make the said Election within Year and Day after the Right
" of Succession happens to be devolved to him, as said is; o-
" therwise the Right of Succession to said Estate of *Pitfirran*,
" Rents, Mails and Duties thereof, shall, from thenceforth, in-
" continent after expiring of the said Year and Day, devolve,
" accresce, and pertain to the said *James*, and the Heirs sub-
" stitute to him."

The like Proviso is repeated in the Event of the two Estates
happening to unite in the Person of any other of the Substitutes, to whom the like Election is given, of holding and retaining either of the two Estates they should think proper;
and denuding of the other, in favours of the next Substitute;
and the whole of these Clauses, respecting the Junction of the
two Estates, and Devolution of the one or the other, are so
anxiously conceived, as denote the most *enixa voluntas*, that
neither the Right nor the Possession should be united in one

Person,

[4]

Perſon, in order to preſerve and maintain a ſeparate Repreſen-
tation of the two Families.

Proviſo 3d, " That it ſhall not be leiſome or lawful to the
" ſaid *Peter Wedderburn*, or any of the remanent Heirs of Tail-
" zie, *to do any Fact or Deed whatſoever, directly or indirectly, in*
" *any ſort, whereby to alter, infringe, or innovate this preſent*
" *Tailzie, in the Order of Succeſſion, and under the Conditions and*
" *Proviſions above ſpecified, otherwiſe not only any ſuch Facts and*
" *Deeds, ſhall be,* ipſo facto, *void and null, without any Decla-*
" *rator for that Effect :* But alſo, the Contraveener, AND THE
" HEIRS OF THE CONTRAVEENER'S BODY, *ſhall amit,*
" *loſe and tine the ſaid Lands and Eſtate, above written, and the*
" *ſame ſhall, incontinent after the Contravention, fall, accreſce and*
" *pertain to the next immediate Heir, ſubſtitute to the Contraveener,*
" *to whom it ſhall be lawful,* &c."

Proviſo 4th, " But Prejudice to the ſaid *Peter Wedderburn*,
" and haill remanent Heirs of Tailzie and Subſtitution above
" written, in their Order of Succeſſion above expreſſed, *of the*
" *Fee, full free Right and Property of the ſaid Lands and Eſtate*
" *above written, whereby it is and ſhall be lawful to them, to*
" *ſell and annailzie the ſame, or any Part thereof, for onerous*
" *Cauſes, and thereupon to contract and on-take Debts, Wadſets,*
" *Infeftments of Annualrent, or other real Rights and Securities*
" *to grant, and all other Facts and Deeds thereanent to do, uſe,*
" *and exerce, at their Pleaſure, providing the ſame be not done*
" *gratuitouſly, or of Deſign and Intention to fruſtrate this pre-*
" *ſent Tailzie, and Deſtination of the Order of Succeſſion above*
" *written, or the Conditions above expreſſed, adjected thereto in any*
" *ſort ;* hereby declaring, that it ſhall be lawful to the next
" immediate Heir-ſubſtitute, to impugn, quarrel, or reduce
" any ſuch Deeds, made gratuitouſly, or of Deſign to fruſtrate,
" as ſaid is ; *which being ſo found and declared, the ſame ſhall in-*
" *fer a direct Contravention againſt the Granter, who, and the*
" *Heirs of the Granter's Body, ſhall thereby tine the Right of the*
" *ſaid*

" said Lands and Eſtate, and the ſame ſhall, incontinent thereafter,
" accreſce and devolve in Manner above provided."

From this Settlement, of the Tenor above recited, your
Lordſhips will obſerve, that the only Limitations impoſed upon the Heirs of Proviſion, were, 1ſt, The carrying the Name
and Arms. 2dly, That they ſhould do no gratuitous Deeds,
of Deſign and Intention to fruſtrate the Deſtination and Order
of Succeſſion, but that, in all other Reſpects, they were unlimited Fiars, and were left at full Liberty to ſell the Eſtate,
or to charge it with Debts to whatever Extent, and to do all
other Facts and Deeds thereanent, at their Pleaſure. 3dly,
That, in caſe of Contravention, the Contraveener irritated
the Right, not only for himſelf, but for all the Deſcendents of
his Body.

Of even Date with the Tailzie laſt abovementioned, Sir
Peter Wedderburn executed the like Settlement of his Eſtate of
Goſford, identically the ſame, mutatis mutandis, with this only
Difference, that, in reſpect the Eſtate of Pitfirran ſtood pro-
vided to Peter, the eldeſt Son, and the Heirs of his Body, he
and his Iſſue were not called to the Succeſſion of the Eſtate of
Goſford, but upon the Failure of the whole other Iſſue of his
Father, and all their Deſcendents ; and the Eſtate of Goſford
was thereby limited, in the firſt place, to Charles, the ſecond
Son, and the Heirs male and female of his Body ; and failing
theſe, to Sir Peter's other younger Children, male and female,
and the Heirs male and female of their reſpective Bodies.

In virtue of theſe Settlements, the Eſtate of Pitfirran, upon
the Death of Sir Peter and his Lady, devolved upon their eldeſt Son Peter, (the late Sir Peter Halket) and the Eſtate of
Goſford devolved on Charles Wedderburn, the ſecond Son.

Peter, during the Lifetime of his Father, intermarried with
Lady Emilia Stewart, ſecond Daughter to Francis Earl of
Moray, and by the poſtnuptial Marriage-contract, of this Date,
Sir Peter and his ſaid Son, became bound and obliged, and there-
by granted Procuratory for reſigning the Eſtate of Pitfirran,
in favours, and for new Infeftment of the ſame, to be made

Sept. 9,
1706.

Feb. 15,
and 17,
1738.

B

and

and granted to the said *Peter Halket* himself, and failing him by Decease, to the Heirs-male already procreated or to be procreated between him and the said Lady *Emilia Stewart*, and the Heirs whatsoever of their Bodies; whom failing, to the Heirs-male of the said Sir *Peter Halket*'s Body, in any subsequent Marriage, and the Heirs whatsoever of their Bodies; whom failing, to the Daughters or Heirs-female of said Marriage, in their Order of Seniority, and the Heirs whatsoever of their Bodies; whom failing, in favours of the Heirs of Tailzie substitute, and Successors appointed to succeed to said Estate, by the Bond and Deed of Tailzie thereof, granted by the deceased Dame *Janet Halket*, 9th *September* 1706, and with and under the Provisions, Conditions, Limitations, and Restrictions therein contained. From all which it is apparent, that as the Settlement, contained in this Marriage-contract, was no other than a Renewal or Repetition of the former Settlement in the Tailzie 1706, no additional Limitations or Restraints were imposed by the one, beyond what was contained in the other, further than as it is implied in every Marriage-settlement, whereby a Succession is provided to the Heir of the Marriage, that the Father shall do no fraudulent gratuitous Deed, in prejudice and defraud of that Provision.

Of this Marriage, between the late Sir *Peter Halket* and Lady *Emilia Stewart*, there were Issue procreated two Sons, *Peter* the eldest, now Sir *Peter Halket*, and *Francis*, the second.

Peter, the eldest of these two Sons, was, from his Birth, a natural Idiot, destitute of the smallest Particles of Reason, Judgment, or Understanding, in so much that, by the afflicting Hand of Providence, he was void of most natural Instincts common to Mankind, and the Brute Creation.

This was a distressing Circumstance to Sir *Peter Halket*, the Father of this unfortunate Youth, and which was greatly increased from the Consideration, that he was to be the Representative of his Family, supposing him to be capable of such Representation. His parental Fondness restrained him, for a long time, from taking any Measures towards a Settlement of the Estate,

in

in the View of this melancholy Profpect ; but, at length, he refolved to do, what it is believed every Parent, in his unfortunate Situation, would have done, and which every Man, who brings the Cafe home to himfelf, muft approve of, that is, of making a new Settlement of the Eftate, identically the fame, in every refpect, with the former Settlement, with this only Difference, of pafling over his eldeft Son, and fettling the fame upon his fecond.

Accordingly, of this Date, he granted a Procuratory for re-figning faid Eftate of *Pitfirran, for fundry weighty Caufes and Confiderations him thereto moving,* in favours and for new Infeftment thereof to himfelf, and failing him, by deceafe, to *Francis Halket* his fecond Son, and the Heirs whatfoever of his Body ; whom failing, to a *Series* of other Subftitutes, precifely the fame with thofe in the Settlement of that Eftate in the 1706, and under the Provifions, Conditions, and Irritancies therein contained. *[marginal note: Octob. 14, 1751.]*

The weighty Caufes and Confiderations which induced him to make that Settlement in favours of his fecond Son, pafling by the eldeft, were feelingly exprefled in a Bond of Aliment and Annuity, executed of the fame Date, *viz.* the natural Imbecillity and total Deprivation of Judgment of his eldeft Son, in refpect of which he thereby fecured him in an alimentary Annuity of 100 *l. Sterling,* payable to the Truftees therein named, to be applied for his Aliment and Suftenance ; and, in order to remove fo diftrefling an Object from his and his Mother's Eyes, he placed him in the Royal Infirmary of this City, where he would be more properly taken care of, and where he ftill remains a natural Idiot, as he was from his Birth deftitute of every Spark of Judgment or Reafon, though he is now above thirty Years of Age.

Upon the Procuratory of Refignation, contained in this laft mentioned Deed, a Charter under the Great Seal was expede, whereupon Sir *Peter* and his Son *Francis* were infeft, and after Sir *Peter*'s Death, his Son *Francis* poffefled the Eftate, without Challenge, to his Death in *November* 1760.

Charles

[8]

Charles Wedderburn, the second Son of old Sir *Peter Halket*, succeeded to the Estate of *Gosford* under the abovementioned Settlement of that Estate, and left several Children, particularly Captain *John Wedderburn* now of *Gosford*, his eldest Son, *Henry* his second Son, now in the *East Indies*, and several others.

By the Death of *Francis Halket*, last of *Pitfirran*, without Issue, and supposing his eldest Brother, the Idiot, to be either incapable, or rightly excluded from the Succession of that Estate, by his Father's Settlement above recited, the Succession to that Estate devolves upon Captain *John Wedderburn* of *Gosford*; but as he cannot hold both Estates, and must denude of the one or the other, in favours of his younger Brother, *Henry*, now in the *East Indies*, and the other Substitutes in their Order, and amongst these in favours of *Alexander Wedderburn*, now of *St. Germains*, the only surviving younger Brother of the late Sir *Peter Halket*, a Scheme seems to have been devised to prevent the Separation of these two Estates, at least, during the Lifetime of the present Sir *Peter Halket*, the Idiot, and to continue Captain *Wedderburn* in the Enjoyment of the Rents of saids Estates, if not in his own Right, at least in Name of the Idiot, as Administrator in Law to him.

In this View, Captain *Wedderburn* took out a Brieve of Idiotry from his Majesty's Chancery, and having adduced before the Jury, composed of Gentlemen of distinguished Characters and Abilities, a most full and distinct Proof of Sir *Peter*'s being a natural Idiot, and totally deprived of Judgment, from his Infancy downwards, he obtained an unanimous Verdict, whereby the Persons of Inquest " Cognosced, serv-
" ed and declared, the said Sir *Peter Halket*, *incompos mentis*,
" fatuous, and a natural Idiot, and that he has been so from
" his Infancy; and that the said Captain *John Wedderburn* is
" his nearest Agnat, &c."

Matters being thus prepared, Captain *Wedderburn* was pleased to bring a Process of Reduction, in Name of the said Sir *Peter Halket*, and of the said Captain *Wedderburn* himself, as

his

his Curator in Law, wherein he called himfelf, and the other Subftitutes under the above mentioned Deeds of Settlement, as Defenders, calling for Production of the Procuratory of Refignation and Deed of Tailzie therein contained, of the Eftate of *Pitfirran*, granted by the late Sir *Peter Halket*, in favours of his fecond Son *Francis*, and other Subftitutes therein mentioned, and to hear and fee the fame, with all that had followed thereon, reduced, as being contrary to, and in Defraud of the Settlement of that Eftate, in favours of the prefent Sir *Peter Halket*, both by the original Tailzie 1706, and his Father and Mother's Contract of Marriage 1738, and in manifeft Contravention of the expreffed and implied Prohibitions in both thefe Settlements.

Henry Wedderburn, the younger Brother of Captain *Wedderburn* of *Gosford*, the Perfon more immediately interefted in the Defence of this Procefs, as the Devolution of one or other of thefe Eftates muft firft operate in his favours, being at the Time abroad in the *Eaft Indies*, Compearance was made for *Alexander Wedderburn* of *St. Germains*, one of the Subftitutes, and fundry Defences were pleaded in bar of this Reduction, which being argued in Prefence, your Lordfhips were pleafed to fuperfede giving Judgment until the next Seffion, and in the mean time, directed both Parties to lodge Informations, in Obedience to which, this is humbly offered on the Part of *Alexander Wedderburn* of *St. Germains*, for Behoof of the whole Subftitutes, and more particularly of his Nephew, the faid *Henry Wedderburn*, who ftands firft in Order.

The Defences, which are now to be fubmitted to your Lordfhips Confideration, refolve into the following Particulars, *1ft*, The Incapacity of the prefent Sir *Peter Halket*, to take any Eftate in this Country by Succeffion, in refpect of his being cognofced and found, by the aforefaid Verdict, which is *probatio probata*, to be now, and to have been from his Infancy, a natural Idiot. *2dly*, That in refpect thereof, and notwith-

C

ftanding

ftanding the general Prohibition in the original Tailzie of this
Eſtate, whereby the ſeveral Heirs of Entail were reſtrained
from doing gratuitous Deeds, of Deſign and Intention to
fruſtrate ſaid Tailzie, and the Deſtination of Succeſſion therein
contained, the late Sir *Peter Halket* was entitled to paſs over
his ſaid eldeſt Son, and to ſettle the Eſtate upon his ſecond
Son, and the other Subſtitutes in their Order, and did not
thereby counteract the Spirit and Intendment of that Prohibition. 3*dly*, That if the late Sir *Peter* ſhall be ſuppoſed to
have thereby counteracted the Prohibition, he incurred the
Irritancy, and thereby forfeited the Eſtate, both for himſelf
and his Iſſue, which, upon that Suppoſition, would devolve
upon Captain *Wedderburn* of *Gosford*, the next Subſtitute, but
who could not hold both Eſtates; ſo that in either View, he
behoved to denude of one or other of theſe Eſtates, in favours
of the other Subſtitutes in their Order.

And with reſpect to the *firſt* of theſe, *viz.* The legal Incapacity of a natural Idiot, to ſucceed to any Land-eſtate in
this Country, it is neceſſary to diſtinguiſh between that total
Deprivation of Judgment, which accompanies thoſe unhappy
Objects from their Birth, which anſwers to the legal Deſcrip-
tion of a natural Idiot, and the ſame Degree of Incapacity,
ariſing from external or ſupervenient Cauſes, whereby thoſe
who were formerly endowed with Reaſon, are by the afflicting
Hand of Providence deprived thereof.

Where Inſanity or Idiotry, proceeds from any ſuch external
Cauſe, the ſame Providence that inflicted can relieve, and
many Inſtances have occurred, where ſuch Perſons have been
reſtored to the Uſe of their Reaſon. In ſuch Caſes it is juſtly
conſidered to be the ſame, in every Reſpect, as any other Diſ-
temper incident to human Nature, which, proceeding from
external Cauſes, the Effects thereof may ceaſe, without Miracles, or any uncommon Interpoſition of Providence; and
however preſumptuous it would be, to ſet Bounds to what
Providence can do, yet as Miracles have long ago ceaſed, as

human

human Laws cannot be regulated by such mere Possibilities, and as no Instance has occurred, since the Creation of the World to this Day, so far as the Defenders ever heard, where a natural Idiot did ever attain the Use of Reason; human Laws must hold it to be an invariable Principle in Natural Philosophy, that he is absolutely incapable thereof, without a new Creation, by an extraordinary Interposition of Providence.

The contrary Principle would run into numberless Absurdities, if human Laws were to be regulated by what Almighty Providence can do. The complete Formation of a Child *in utero*, is by Nature circumscribed to the Space of nine Months, or thereby; upon this are founded the Laws of all Nations, respecting Legitimacy, or the *status liberorum*, and civil Rights depending thereon; no Man can be so presumptuous as to say, that Providence may not continue the *fœtus in utero*, for nine Years, or bring it to Perfection in nine Days, instead of nine Months. But it would surely be a most extraordinary Argument, if these bare Possibilities, or what Providence can do by Miracles, or other extraordinary Interpositions, were to influence human Laws.

And where that is the Case, the Defenders, in the Argument upon this first Point, will hold it for certain, *præsumptione juris et de jure*, that as this nominal Pursuer is proved, and by the unanimous Verdict of this respectful Inquest, cognosced and found to be a natural Idiot, and to have been such from his Infancy, he will, and must remain such while he lives, and every Question respecting this Matter, must be judged upon that Supposition.

And so far as the Defenders have been able to discover, no Instance has occurred, where a natural Idiot, so previously found and cognosced, was attempted to be served and retoured Heir upon the Brieve of Mortanceſtry, which is one of the strongest negative Evidences, that they were deemed incapable of such Right, and if any Instances of this Kind could be produced,

duced, it muft have proceeded *per incuriam,* or the Jury's having no Evidence of the Fact laid before them. Incidental Idiotry is a very different Matter; it is, as already faid, no other than a Diftemper, the Caufe of which being removed, the Judgment may return, of which there have been many Inftances; fo that in fuch Cafe, to deny the Perfon, afflicted with fuch Diftempers, the Enjoyment of any civil Right, or a Capacity to take and hold the fame, would be carrying the Confequences beyond the Caufe.

The Brieve of Mortanceftry was chiefly intended for the fpecial Services of Heirs in thofe Lands, wherein their Predeceffors died laft veft and feafed, and fuch continues to be the Tenor of all thofe Brieves down to this Day, even when a general Service is only intended, which is the Child of the fpecial Service.

And as the Ward-holding, is the proper and ancient Tenure of all Lands, where the Inveftiture is not otherways conceived, it became one Head of the Brieve of Mortanceftry, whether the Claimant was of lawful Age, which, if no other Incapacity fuperveened, the Law fixed to be his Age of twenty-one; and therefore, during his Minority, when held incapable to perform the Services of Ward-holding, returned the Lands into the Hands of the Superior, to the end that he might provide one that was capable to perform the Duty; fo that by that Head of the Brieve, refpecting his being of lawful Age, was clearly underftood his being of Capacity to enter upon the Feu, and to difcharge the Duties thereof. With what Propriety that Head of the Brieve could be anfwered of a natural Idiot, muft be humbly fubmitted.

Sir *Thomas Craig,* in *Lib.* 2. *Dieg.* 18. § where he treats, *De his quæ impediunt fucceffionem,* clearly embraces this Diftinction, and holds a natural Idiot to be incapable of fuch Succeffion. His Words are: " Sextum impedimentum eft " imperfectio, et quicunque ob naturalem mentis qualitatem " imperfecti nafcuntur, in his hæc generalis regula fervanda

" eft,

" eft, quod in hac naturali imperfectione, tempus fucceffionis
" femper infpiciendum."

In the feudal Law, it was a Doubt whether fuch bodily Im-
perfections, as rendered the Heir of the Vaffal abfolutely incapable to perform the Duties of the Ward-holding, fuch as
Blindnefs, Deafnefs, &c. were not fufficient, *per fe*, to ex-
clude him from the Right of fucceeding to fuch Eftate; and
if that was but a doubtful Point, it could not furely admit of
a Queftion, whether a natural Idiot had fuch Capacity.

Nor is it indeed eafy to conceive, how human Laws could
mean to render fuch a Being capable of any civil Right. It
is not the Form and Figure of the Body, that conftitutes a
Man: The legal, as well as the philofophical Definition of
him is, *quod fit animal rationale*. When God Almighty cre-
ated Man after his own Image, it was not the external or
human Body, but the inward Man, that refembled the Divi-
nity; and therefore, as a human Body without Judgment,
can never compofe that rational Being, which conftitutes the
Man, a Perfon naturally devoid of all Reafon, is no Man in
the Senfe of Law, or the common Underftanding of Mankind. He is no better than any other of the Brute Creation,
and therefore cannot be confidered as coming under the general Defcription of Heirs of any kind, in the Settlement of
any Eftate. He may anfwer the Defcription, in fo far as he
is procreated of fuch Perfons, or the Iffue of fuch Marriage,
but he is not fuch Being as could poffibly be intended, or in
the View of Parties, and therefore no general Words will apply to him. He is not the complete Man, and the Character
of Heir can apply to no other.

Suppofing the Cafe of a Monfter being produced, and fuch
miferable Inftances have occurred, that Creature would be the
Iffue of the Marriage, the firft born; but he would not be
fuch Iffue as could poffibly be intended to fucceed; and a human Body, deprived of Reafon from its firft Production, no
more anfwers the Character of a rational Creature, than any

D

Monfter

Monfter in Nature. The Words may favour both, but the Intendment applies to neither; and, in that Refpect, it is fubmitted to your Lordfhips, whether this natural Idiot had any fuch Right to this Eftate, as can found him in the Challenge, which is now made of his Father's Settlement.

The *fecond* Point, propofed for your Lordfhips Confideration, proceeds upon Suppofition of the Purfuer's natural Capacity to take this Eftate, under the above mentioned Deeds of Settlement. And the Queftion from thence arifing is, Whether the Prohibition, of the Tenor above recited, is to be fo Judaically interpreted, as to have incapacitated the late Sir *Peter Halket*, upon this unlooked-for Misfortune of his eldeft Son, being a natural Idiot, to pafs him over, and give the Eftate to the fecond Son?

That every Man, in Sir *Peter's* unhappy Situation, with refpect to his eldeft Son, with a moft upright Intention, and without meaning to violate or fruftrate the Settlement of the Eftate, would have attempted to do what Sir *Peter* in this Cafe did; and that all the impartial World muft approve of the Meafures he took, fuppofing him not to have thereby exceeded his Powers, is a Propofition felf-evident, and which every Man muft feel, that brings the Cafe home to himfelf; nothing could be more proper to anfwer the chief Purpofe of the Settlements of thefe two Eftates, *viz.* that they fhould always be kept feparate, fo that each Family might have a diftinct Reprefentation. This was the grand Object in View by both Settlements. How well that would be anfwered, by the Reprefentation of a natural Idiot, needs no Illuftration.

It is impoffible to imagine, that when, by the Settlement of this Eftate, the fame was devifed to a *Series* of Heirs, under general Defcriptions, as procreated of the Body of this Perfon or that Perfon, it could be in the View of the Devifer to comprehend therein natural Idiots. Every Man's Reafon muft revolt againft fuch an abfurd Suppofition. How could a natural Idiot be fuppofed capable of complying with any of the Conditions

ditions required by that Tailzie? Or, how could he incur any of the Irritancies thereby imposed, in case of Contravention? The whole of the Settlement, and these Clauses in particular, did necessarily suppose a Capacity in that Person that was to take under that Settlement; and therefore, it can be no Counter-action of the Prohibition, when such Being is past by, and the Estate continued in the same Line of Succession, excluding him.

This Construction is strongly justified from the Words of the Clause itself, which vests every Heir of Entail with an unlimited Fee, with this single Exception, that he do no Deed, merely gratuitous, of design and intention to frustrate the Tailzie and Destination of Succession therein contained. The Settlement which the late Sir *Peter Halket* made, may be deemed gratuitous, because no valuable Consideration was given for his executing the same; but it was not so done, of design and intention to frustrate the Succession thereby established; on the contrary, it was done with an honest and fair Intention, to follow out what was understood to be the true and rational Purpose of that Settlement, *viz.* to transmit the Estate to the *Series* of Heirs thereby appointed, one after another, upon supposition, that the Persons thereby appointed to succeed, not by Name, but by general Descriptions, were rational Beings, not natural Idiots.

In every Settlement of this kind, there must be implied Conditions; those that are intrinsick and natural, are as effectual as if expressed. Had this Case occurred to the Maker of the Settlement, it is impossible to doubt, what her Answer would have been; and therefore, whatever Difficulty there may be in destroying a Settlement of this kind, from presumed Intention, yet, as every Case of this kind is a *quæstio voluntatis*, if the Circumstances are such, as must convince every unbiassed Mind, that such could not possibly be the Intendment of the Deed, that Construction ought to be taken, which will reconcile the Words to the Intendment; and the Defenders humbly

humbly fubmit it to your Lordfhips, that the Diftinction already fuggefted, is abundantly fufficient for that Purpofe, *viz.* That, as the Queftion does not refpect the Exclufion of any Perfon *nominatim*, called by the Settlement, but of one that is fuppofed to have been called under a general Defcription, as the Iffue procreated of fuch another Perfon, if that Defcription does neceffarily imply and fuppofe the Perfon fo meant to be called, to be a rational Being, not a natural Idiot, the paffing him by, is no counteracting of what was truly intended by fuch Settlement; and, if there is any feeming Contradiction between the Words and the Intention, the former muft yield to the latter, as the only Ufe of Words is to convey the Meaning of Parties; and no Man, that lays his Hand to his Heart, can fay, that the late Sir *Peter*'s Settlement in 1738, was meant to fruftrate and difappoint the Succeffion of that Eftate, according to the true Spirit and Intendment of the Settlement therein contained.

This Rule of Conftruction has been received in fimilar Cafes. Thus, in particular it is, that general Words, in ftrict Settlements of this Kind, prohibiting the Heirs of Entail from felling or difponing any Part of the entailed Eftate, upon any Caufe or Occafion whatever, has not been fo Judaically interpreted as to reftrain the Heir in Poffeffion from difponing the Eftate to his eldeft Son and apparent Heir in his Marriage-contract, or otherwife, for this plain Reafon, that, by fo doing, he does not counteract the ultimate Scope and Purpofe of the Settlement, when the Difpofition is in favours of the next Heir, though the Prohibition was general, without any fuch Exception.

The fame equitable Confiderations have induced your Lordfhips, as far as poffible, to reftrain the Extravagancies of thefe Settlements, and to keep them within proper Bounds; and if any Liberties of this Kind are to be taken, there cannot be a more favourable Occafion than the prefent, where the only Confequence of the Conftruction contended for, is to recon-

cile

cile the Words of the Deed with the reasonable Purpose and Intendment of it.

For as to any additional Argument arising from the Marriage-contract, the Defenders have already said, and submit it to your Lordships, that that cannot influence the Question one Way or other. It is no other than a Renewal of the same Settlement, upon occasion of the late Sir *Peter Halket*'s Marriage, whereby the Estate was again settled upon the same Heirs, and under the same Conditions as before.

Had there been no previous Tailzie, it cannot admit of a Question, that Sir *Peter*'s Deed of Exclusion of the eldest Son, in respect of his natural Idiotry, would have justified the same. So the Point was judged in a much straiter Case, that of *Douglas* of *Tilliquholly*, 10th *July* 1724, where it was found, That the Father, notwithstanding of the Provision of the Estate in his Contract of Marriage, to the Heir of that Marriage, might, for rational Causes, pass by the eldest Son, and give the Estate to the second Son of the Marriage; and, though that Judgment has generally been disapproven of, in regard of the Insufficiency of these Reasons which weighed with the Father to pass over his eldest Son, the general Rule of Law thereby established, *viz.* that such Exclusion may be upon just Causes, notwithstanding the express Provision in the Marriage-contract, and implied Obligation, to do no Deed in defraud thereof, has, with great Reason been approven of; and if any Case can be figured, where such Exclusion is rational, what can be stronger than the unhappy Situation of the eldest Son, being a natural Idiot.

And this leads to the *third* and *last* Point proposed for your Lordships Consideration, which does not require to be inferred by any Argument. The Pursuer alledges, that his Father, Sir *Peter*, by settling the Estate upon his second Son, counteracted the Prohibition in the Entail, and it is upon that Supposition, that he now brings his Challenge; and the Defender, for Argument's sake, shall hold that to be the Case. What

E

is

is the Confequence ? Neither more nor lefs than that Sir *Peter* did thereby incur the Irritancy, whereby he forfeited the Eftate for himfelf and his Iffue. ·

The Purfuer cannot be permitted to lay hold of the Prohibition, as a Ground for reducing his Father's Deed, and, at the fame time, fhake himfelf loofe of the Confequences of that Contravention. If the Deed is liable to be reduced, as contrary to the Prohibition, your Lordfhips muft find, that Sir *Peter* thereby incurred the Irritancy, both for himfelf and Defcendents; the Confequence of which will be, to carry over the Eftate to Captain *Wedderburn*, who having already taken the Eftate of *Gosford*, cannot hold both Eftates, but muft denude of the one of them in favours of the next Subftitute: So that, in this View of the Cafe, it is truly Matter of Moon-fhine, whether he takes by virtue of the laft Sir *Peter*'s Settlement, or by the Irritancy incurred by Sir *Peter*'s having made that Settlement.

The Purfuer was pleafed to figure Hardfhips and Inconveniencies that might arife, if the Eftate fhould, in the mean time, be fold, or charged with Debt by the Heir in Poffeffion, either of which the Settlement allows him to do, and that Sir *Peter* fhould thereafter be reftored to his Judgment, when he would certainly be intitled to recover the Eftate, fuppofing it to be ftill extant.

But as this Danger is quite chimerical, and of which no one Inftance can be produced fince the Creation of the World, that one, by Nature an Idiot from his firft Exiftence, fhould thereafter acquire the Ufe of Reafon, thofe bare Poffibilities, which would require an extraordinary Interpofition of Providence, are *extra legis obfervantiam*. Nor would it be proper now to difpute, how far the Law would liften to a Claim of this Kind, from a Perfon once fairly laid afide, though, be that as it will, it can give no Aid to this Reduction. Your Lordfhips might poffibly be of opinion, that a tacite *Fideicommiff.* was implied, in cafe the Idiot fhould be reftored to Judgment,

ment, fimilar to what was found in the Cafe of *Mackinnon,* where the after Exiftence of a nearer Heir was found to intitle him to recover the Eftate from the remoter Heir, who had eftablifhed his Titles, and had attained Poffeffion, at a Time when the nearer Heir had no Exiftence.

But it would be cutting before the Point, to argue what ought to be the Judgment of the Law in fuch Cafe. That Queftion will come time enough, when the Cafe happens, which to all human Appearance it never can ; and if Captain *Wedderburn* apprehends any of thofe difmal Confequences with refpect to his particular Concern, he has an eafy Remedy, by retaining his proper Eftate of *Gosford,* and allowing the Eftate of *Pitfirran* to pafs to the next Subftitute, a Meafure he will not probably be difpofed to follow, as the one Eftate is of fo much fuperior Value to the other, though *ob majorem fecuritatem,* he is defirous to have your Lordfhips Judgment, affirming the late Sir *Peter Halket's* Settlement, and the Defenders are willing to think, that this is the fole Purpofe of the prefent Action.

In refpect whereof, &c.

ALEX. LOCKHART.